FROM SIDE HUSTLES
TO FORTUNE 500

THE STARTUP KING
From Side Hustles to Fortune 500

BEAR AFKHAMI

Editor: Jamie Wiesner
Cover Art: Elizabeth Huber

ISBN: 9781549674860

Contents

Preface on the American Dream

For centuries the defining American experience, whether through literature, music, science, technology or politics, has always centered on the American dream. Literature's beloved protagonists begin in a childhood struggle for food and end surrounded by mansions, money and success. Our favorite musicians hustle on the street for years rhyming about their struggles to finally make it into multi-millionaires. Our great American scientists, hindered by other nations, use the American freedom to innovate and invent. Our titans of technology begin their multi-billion dollar corporations in the family garage and change the world.

The American dream and the pursuit of happiness intersect with the spirit of American entrepreneurism. Our American heroes, musicians, scientists and titans of industry share these common characteristics. Entrepreneurism is baked in our culture. Taking financial risk to realize gains runs deep in our veins. Working day and night to better our position in life comes naturally to Americans, so much so that some consider this privilege, to hustle and thrive, the real American dream.

Why do so many Americans consider the mere ability to work hard and thrive such a privilege? Simply put, the United States is one of the only places in the world where hard work has the chance to change your standing. As a first generation immigrant, I can attest that America, unlike much of the rest of the world, is a place full of opportunity. This opportunity is what motivated my mother and father to bring my brother and me to the United States. They embraced opportunity fully and worked day and night to build the American Dream for our family. For this and the example of hard work they set, I am eternally grateful.

"The Startup King" is my effort to continue my family's appreciation for opportunity and the American Dream by helping other hardworking Americans realize their startup dreams.

Introduction

According to World Bank data, out of 190 countries in the world, the United States ranks eight[1] in what they refer to as the "Ease of Doing Business Rank." This ranking aggregates such factors as the number of procedures to start a business, the time in days it takes to start a business and the cost associated with starting a business (measured in percentage of income per capita). It also includes, but is not limited such factors as registering property, getting credit, paying taxes, enforcing contracts and more.

While many expect America to be number one in this ranking, and of course we should strive to be, we should also recognize that we are lucky to be presented with this privilege and opportunity to start a business easily. Why wait another day? Take advantage of this opportunity and start a business! You have ideas that could turn into the next great product. You have skills that can make you into the next great business owner and community leader. Or maybe you just have some spare energy to turn into extra money for your next vacation, home or retirement.

Whether you are ready for your side hustle while you work a full time job, have always dreamt of being your own boss, or want to turn your brilliant idea into a cash cow, this book can help you startup your business correctly from the start.

"The Startup King" is a culmination of more than ten years of startup consulting experience working and helping small businesses and entrepreneurs. It also includes hundreds of hours of research in business planning, marketing, entity formation, bookkeeping, administrative support, payroll, human resources and purchasing best practices.

"The Startup King" shares simple processes and practical advice for anyone who is thinking about starting a business or is already a startup entrepreneur. The goal of this book is to make the startup process as efficient and simple as possible, by answering an extensive list of frequently asked questions, explaining startup processes and providing detailed checklists to keep startup entrepreneurs organized. While the content in this book is extensive, remember that every situation is unique. You should always do your due diligence and consult with an attorney before making legal decisions such as starting a business.

What this book does NOT cover: "The Startup King" does not cover the processes, albeit similar to a business, of starting a non-profit entity. The book is also NOT a form of legal advice and you should most definitely check your local and state laws before making decisions. Finally, this book does NOT aim to give you ideas on the types of businesses you could start.

1

General Startup Advice

This is it!

This year will be THE year that you're going to become your own boss. "The Startup King" welcomes you to the club with the following seven points of advice.

1. Understand and accept that it's going to be hard. The startup process, when done correctly, will be hard, and keeping the business going for the initial one to three years is going to be harder. It will be hard on you, your family and your lifestyle. You will doubt yourself, but don't give up. Even companies like Google took longer than five years to become profitable.

2. It's scary. Doing something new and being the person responsible for all decisions is outside the comfort zone of most people. You have to come to terms with this and actively remind yourself to be brave. Oftentimes you can find hundreds of excuses to convince yourself that it's not a good time to go out on your own. Remember that you just need one good reason to push yourself into realizing your entrepreneurial dreams.

3. Take advantage of strategic drawbacks in order to accomplish your startup goals. Some of the most accomplished leaders and successful entrepreneurs in history have strategically scaled back their lifestyle in order to achieve their larger goals. If you need to move back in with your parents to put the money into your business, do it, but do so with strategic purpose and planning.

4. Do something you care about. If you're going to be your own boss and be scared and stressed everyday, you might as well invest all that energy into something you love to do or care deeply about. This doesn't have to be a type of profession or cause, but something like working with a group of people with whom you'd like to spend time.

5. You don't have to quit your day job immediately. If you're being paid well for your time, you should make a strategic decision to spend as long as possible at your day job, while working on your startup on the side. Again, this will be hard and stressful, but a good decision if done correctly and strategically.

6. You need a written plan, but don't waste time with a 100-page business plan loaded with corporate speak and business jargon. That's a waste of time and often serves as a deterrent to startup. Your first business plan should be aimed at yourself and in outline format. Make sure to include a checklist of all the things you need to do for your startup, an honest cost evaluation, an honest revenue model and a marketing task plan. Don't worry, "The Startup King" helps with this!

7. Make sure you consult with an expert who has gone through the startup process before. It may seem self-serving to give this advice to startup entrepreneurs, but I have spent quite a bit of time correcting small mistakes that my clients made during their startup process. It may involve small costs initially, but the time that you would save in learning how to start a business, dealing with all the paperwork, writing a business plan, filing all the paperwork with the local/state governments and the IRS, setting up your bookkeeping, accounts payable and receivable process would be well worth it. Spending all that time with the startup process would keep you from concentrating on the part of the business that actually generates revenue. Startup experts know how to do things quickly and also have experience in finding capital through commercial and government programs.

2

Types of Startup Businesses

First things first, there are three different ways to start a business. Let's call them the Side Hustle, the Big Spender and the Ground Up. I'll explain the basics of how each works, then rate them Low, Moderate or High on three factors. Those factors are Risk, Energy required and Investment (in terms of money) required.

With each type of business I'll present you with a checklist to make sure you understand important considerations as you decide what type of startup best suits your situation.

Risk, Energy and Investment Comparison

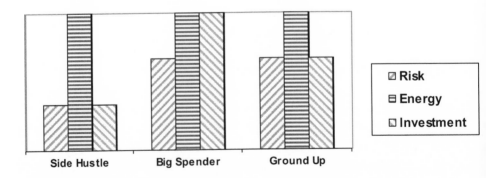

Notice that all three ways of starting a business require a high level of energy!

The Side Hustle

Side Hustlers have their blue or white collar day jobs. Before you go to work, after you come home and on the weekends, you're making extra money doing something that interests you.

Side hustling requires quite a bit of energy because you are engaged with work all day and even all week. But, done right, it can make a good chunk of change and even lead to a full time startup.

- **Risk Factor:** *Low*

    Hey, you already have a job and stable source of income. Maybe it's not your dream or doesn't pay enough, but it's OK. You don't have to go all in to startup.

- **Energy Factor:** *High*

    Hustler's hustle, and as cool as that sounds, it's pretty exhausting hustling so hard for so long. Your day job performance might be impacted and so might your family or social relationships.

- **Investment Factor:** *Low*

    Depending on what your side hustle is, it will typically utilize equipment and space you already have.

The Side Hustle Checklist

- ✓ Pick a side hustle that doesn't legally interfere with your day job. For example, if your day job is selling wine to bars, your side hustle should not be selling a type of wine that your day job doesn't sell. You'll get yourself into quite a bit of legal trouble. Save this type of competition for the Ground Up startup.

- ✓ Pick a side hustle that doesn't clash schedules with your day job. If you work a nine to five, you're not going to be able to meet with your side hustle clients during the day. Don't rob time from your employer.

✓ Pick something you're really good at already. You don't have time as a side hustler to learn a new trade. If you're good at graphic design, coding, selling, etc. that's what you should consider.

✓ Pick something in demand. Just because you're good at it, it doesn't mean people want to pay for it.

✓ Be cost competitive. You've got low startup costs; you have a day job, offer your Side Hustle for less.

The Big Spender

Let's go shopping ... for a business. There is no shortage of websites, services and agencies that advertise the sale of existing businesses. You can get a business broker who will search for you, or you can go solo and search yourself. Either way, you or your broker will contact any businesses up for sale; you sign a confidentiality agreement, tour the business, take a good look at their books (this is where an expert comes in handy) and see how the business works.

If you like what you see, and you think you can either keep the business going or even make it bigger, then you arrange payment, get financing, write a check, hand off a suitcase full of cash, and start.

- **Risk Factor:** *Moderate*

    Assuming you do your research and buy a stable business with a stable history and stable future, you'll just have to make sure you maintain the status quo.

- **Energy Factor:** *High*

    It takes a lot of time to learn how someone else did business, and takes even longer to put your own flare on it. This requires long days and sleepless nights.

- **Investment Factor:** *High*

    Make sure you either have money or be able to secure financing. Buying an existing business will be expensive.

The Big Spender Checklist

- ✓ Find a good business broker to search for you. These guys do it all the time, so they can do it more efficiently. Give them as many details about the type of business you want to buy and run.

- ✓ Don't rely on a broker to tell you if this business is for you. The broker will get paid when you buy the business, so they are motivated to close the deal as soon as possible.

17

✓ Get a Certified Public Accountant (CPA) to review the bookkeeping and tax records of the business WITH you. You need to learn this business from the start, have them explain everything. Their recommendation is very valuable.

✓ Look at the businesses' future potential. Are you looking at a book store? There's not much growth there. Are you looking at a plumbing company where there are hundreds of competing plumbing companies? If the business has future contracts on the books, it is a good sign.

✓ Why is the current owner selling the company? Sure, maybe it's time for them to retire (which is the reason most sellers provide), but maybe their industry has no future or they are tired of working twelve hours a day, seven days a week. Maybe their store is in a high-crime neighborhood, driving insurance costs up too high.

✓ How long is the current owner willing to stay on to teach you the business? Be careful, because sometimes the owner is not the expert in the company that you need to stay on. Sometimes the worker-bee is the star you need by your side.

✓ Make sure you've negotiated a clear "non-compete" agreement as part of your purchasing documents. You must be careful to prevent the current owner of the business you are about to purchase from starting another company conducting the same business. Negotiate how many years the owner will refrain from doing the same business, geographical limitations and be clear about the nature of work prohibited.

The Ground Up

Roll up your sleeves because you're building a foundation, and then everything else on top of it. You don't have a day job and you didn't buy an existing business. You have a vision and you're starting from ground zero. With a clean slate you'll start everything from administrative to legal and financial. Then you'll go out and find customers and do the work.

You should be the expert in the business you will startup.

- **Risk Factor:** *Moderate*
  You have no day job; you have no existing business history. It's just you, your vision and how you run the company.

- **Energy Factor:** *High*
  It will take a lot of time to build a business from the ground up and oversee it all. This requires long days and sleepless nights.

- **Investment Factor:** *Moderate*
  You're not going to be writing one big check, but you need to have capital available to keep you going until the payments from customers start to roll in. That could be months to years depending on what you do.

The Ground Up Checklist

✓ Are you an expert in the field in which you're starting? If you are not, then find another business. Sure, you can find experts, but it's expensive and turnover is high.

✓ Do you have enough capital to keep the lights on until the revenue starts to roll in? If not, you may have to wait, save up, or stick it out with a Side Hustle.

✓ Have you done enough research to make sure there is demand for your company, services or products?

3

Pre-Planning

The pulp of this book, and what I have found that works best for small business startups, is short descriptions and the checklists that you can follow to make sure you do things in the correct order and the most efficiently.

A mini-checklist is offered for each section and a comprehensive checklist is offered in the Appendix of this book. Depending on your level of experience and/or patience, you can go right to the Appendix first, or start here.

***

Let's start with the pre-planning stage of the startup, which includes your Business Plan, Marketing Strategy and if applicable your Operations Agreements.

The saying "If you build it, they will come" from the movie "Field of Dreams" is not very true in the business world. There's absolutely no guarantee that once you start your business, people will flock to your company. It takes good planning and execution to give your business the shot it needs to succeed.

Pre-Planning Checklist

- ☐ Write Business Plan
  - o Write Marketing Strategy
- ☐ Draft Operations Agreement

Business Plan

If you remember earlier in this book I advised you not to waste a lot of time writing a business plan that is dozens of pages long and uses all sorts of corporate jargon. What is a preferable for new startup entrepreneurs is to create guidance and direction with your business plan and then build on it later, when things have started to pick up. For example, when *Amazon.com* founder Jeff Bezos set out to startup the now goliath of online shopping, he wrote his business plan while his wife drove them from New York to Seattle[2].

Keeping this in mind, the Small Business Administration categorizes business plans into two different formats, traditional and lean[3]. You can guess which is recommended by "The Startup King", but let's take a look at the details.

Type of Business Plan	Advantages	Disadvantages
Traditional	• Comprehensive • Detailed • Preferred by lenders and investors	• Takes more time to write • May discourage • May be distracting
Lean	• High-level overview • Fast to write • Key elements only	• Investors may need more details

If this isn't your first time with a startup or if you have some level of business planning experience, then perhaps a Traditional Business Plan might be right for you. Traditional Business Plan components include:

1. **Executive Summary**: What does your company do, sell, service or produce? Why will it be profitable? What makes your business special? What is your mission and vision? If the audience is a lender, imagine that they will only read this portion of the business plan. You must wow them with how unique you are and how much money you'll make. Write your executive summary in a page or less.

2. **Market Analysis:** Who is your target market and what is their future outlook? You must describe your target market with detail and personality, showing that you understand not only who you're targeting, but also their behavior. You will also have to consider how existing businesses target this market and how your company will do it better. Use graphs, charts and color.

3. **Organization and Management:** What is your legal structure and who is the team that will run your company? List the advantages of your chosen legal structure and chart your entire management team, stating what unique experience, skills or knowledge they bring to the business.

4. **Service or Product Line**: What will your business be offering consumers and what is the advantage? Remember to describe the entirety of the life cycle of your product or service. Also, describe any plans to apply for patents and trademarks.

5. **Sales & Marketing:** How are you going to reach customers and sell to them? This section includes a description of sales cycle, your marketing strategy and all the factors that go into it, such as advertising, public relations, etc.

6. **Funding**: What are you asking from lenders or investors? Describe what you will provide in return and in what timeframe profits can be expected. Finally, show how you'll use the money such as buying equipment, paying salaries, opening a store, etc.

7. **Financial Projections:** Lenders will want to see financial projections to show how your business will grow over time. You'll likely have to contact an expert if you're not familiar with how to do this.

8. **Supporting Documents:** Include key personnel resumes, licenses, permits, patents, trademarks, legal documents like entity formations.

Before you start, consider if you have the time and knowledge to dedicate to this endeavor. Also highly consider if you will need to present your traditionally formatted business plan to lenders and investors. If you're not immediately seeking funding, then you're highly encouraged to go with a Lean Business Plan.

The Lean Business Plan is commonly made up for chat formats which include the following categories:

1. **Customer Relationships:** What is the customer's experience with your company from beginning to end? Do you have a method to measure satisfaction and repeat business?
2. **Customer Segments:** Who is your business serving or targeting? Consider demographics, geography, income and other qualitative and quantitative insights.
3. **Channels**: How will you reach your customers?
4. **Cost Structure**: What costs will your company face? Try to be as detailed as possible.
5. **Revenue Streams**: How is your company going to make money? It may be one way, with one product or multiple ways and multiple products.
6. **Key Partnerships**: What suppliers, manufacturers, subcontractors, etc. will you partner with to be competitive?
7. **Key Activities:** What specific factors such as special knowledge, methods or technology, give a competitive advantage to your business?
8. **Key Resources:** What is available to YOU specifically that sets you apart? Is it your staff, access to funding, patent or special business certification?
9. **Value Proposition:** What makes your company unique? You can tie items 6, 7 and 8 altogether here.

Rather than making this book longer, I've refrained from publishing a long form business plan template. Instead I encourage you to visit these two sites for templates on both the Traditional and Lean formats.

For Traditional Business Plan formats, visit the Small Business Administration website by going to www.sba.gov and use the SBA business plan tool.

For Lean Business Plan formats, you can download a template of a form of the lean business plan called the Business Model Canvas, by going directly to strategyzer.com and use the business model canvas.

Operations Agreement

It's not uncommon for a startup entrepreneur to seek help from friends and family. Often friends or family members decide to work together and capitalize on the combining of the mutual resources they bring to the table. If you are one of these entrepreneurs, I highly encourage you to draft an Operations Agreement between all levels of leadership in your company.

Disputes about spending, strategy, hiring and more will arise. It is always best to have established a structure for decision making from the beginning.

You can find or buy an Operations Agreement template online or confer with an attorney to write one for you. At minimum an Operations Agreement should contain details on the following:

1. **Capital Contribution:** How much are each of the partners contributing to the company and how will they be able to withdraw or contribute more?

2. **Banking and Checks**: What bank is being used and which partners will be permitted to withdraw money, deposit, endorse or write checks?

3. **Profits and Losses:** How will profits and losses be distributed?

4. **Prohibited Acts**: Arguably the most important part of the agreement. What actions can one partner not perform with the consent of all or some of the other partners? For example, Partners cannot be involved with any other business, unless agreed to by other partners.

5. **Hiring and Firing**: Who will be in charge of hiring and firing decisions and how many of the partners must agree in order to take action?

6. **Termination of Partnership**: How can one partner leave the partnership?

7. **Right of First Refusal**: If a partner leaves, is he/she required to offer his/her portion of the partnership to the other partners of the company before going outside the company?

8. **Death or Insolvency:** What happens if all or some of the partners die or are no longer able to contribute to the company?

9. **Insurance**: What insurances will be required to be carried?

10. **Holidays and Time Off:** How many days off in can partners take and must they be in equal sums for each partner?

Drafting and signing an Operations Agreement can end up not only helping your business, but also to preserve a long lasting friendship or family relationship.

4

Formation of Entity

The actual creation of your company as a legal entity can be one of the most confusing and exciting stages of the startup process. It is also the stage where many startup entrepreneurs make the most "small mistakes".

In the United States, the entity formation is relatively easy depending on the state in which you live. Many states offer online registrations, while mail-in and fax registrations are offered by others. Of course, companies can also be registered in person. Remember that the World Bank's Doing Business Index ranks the United States as fifty-first (51st), so while we're good, we have some improvements to make, and you'll see this as you start.

Formation of Entity Checklist

- ☐ Select Entity Registration State
    - o Identify Resident Agent(s)
- ☐ Select Entity Type
    - o Sole Proprietorship
    - o Partnership
    - o Corporation
    - o C Corporation / S Corporation / B Corporation
    - o Limited Liability Company
- ☐ Select Post LLC Formation Filing Status
    - ▪ C-Corp OR S-Corp
- ☐ Brainstorm Entity Names
    - o Also Brainstorm "Trade" Names (if applicable)
    - o Check Entity Name Availability with State
    - o Check Entity Trade Name Availability with State

- o Finalize Names
- Draft Articles of Organization
  - o File Articles of Organization (In Person, Online, Fax)
  - o Wait for Confirmation of Acceptance
- Apply for FEIN with IRS
- Apply for State Government Account Numbers
  - o State Withholding Tax Number
  - o State Unemployment Tax Number
  - o State Sales/Use Tax Number (if/when applicable)
- Apply for Local/County Government Account Numbers
  - o Business License Permit
- Identify Need for Special State/Federal Trade License or Permit
  - o Begin Process if Applicable (May Require Attorney)
- Identify Eligibility for State/Federal Special Business Certifications to Qualify for Special Access
- Identify Need for Trademark or Patent Registration (Requires Attorney)
- Foreign Corporation Registrations in Other States

Selecting an Entity Registration State and Picking a Resident Agent

In the United States, companies are registered by state governments and then recognized by the federal government. During the registration process and regardless of where your startup is registered, you must declare a resident agent, who will receive all communications from the state government on your behalf. The resident agent MUST be a resident of that state. Of course, the resident agent can always be one of the owners of the business.

So, where should you register your startup? You may be asking, isn't the obvious choice to register my company in the state in which I live? While that may seem obvious and very often the right choice, you should consider registration in another state because of the benefits to your business.

According to a *legalzoom®* article, if you own a home, have a physical office or storefront location and the majority of your business is done in your home state, then it is likely that you must register your company in your home state[4]. If you do not have a physical location, such as consultants, and the majority of your business is outside your home state, then it may be more advantageous to register in another state.

	Advantages	Disadvantages
Home State	• Convenience • Save money on registration and annual fees • Save money on "Resident Agent"	• State income taxes might be higher
Foreign State	• May save on state income taxes, capital gains and inheritance • Special business courts in other states	• Must find, maintain and pay a Resident Agent

Most entrepreneurs considering registration in a state other than their home state are persuaded to do so with very business-friendly states. Three states in particular are at the top of the list for being cozy with startups. They include Delaware, Nevada and Wyoming. If you are interested in this avenue, take your time to conduct extensive research and consult an attorney specializing in corporate tax law to help you with your decision.

In both home state and foreign state registrations, it is always wise to have an attorney or a business consultant review your filing documents prior to your filing. Remember that if you are based in one state and have employees in others, you are likely required to register as a Foreign State Entity in those other states.

Selecting an Entity Type

Selecting the type of legal entity for your business is an important matter as it impacts how you are liable for your business practices, the number of tax obligations as well as the number and types of filings with state and federal governments. It is best to choose correctly from the startup to avoid costly changes in the future. It is best to consult an attorney or business consultant.

There are seven general types of entities for the formation of a startup.

- **Sole Proprietorship**: If tomorrow you started making baskets and selling them, without registering a business, then you would be considered a Sole Proprietorship. While it is easy to choose this entity type, you and your business are treated as one and there is no separation between your personal and business assets or liabilities.
- **Partnership**: There are limited partnerships (LP) and limited liability partnerships (LLP). In the former, LP, there is one general partner with unlimited liability and the rest of the partners are limited liability partners with less control of the company. In the latter, LLP, all partners have limited liability. Keep in mind that other entities will also offer options for groups wanting to start a business.
- **Corporation**: There are three different types of corporations (C Corp, S Corp and B Corp). Corporations offer complete separation from their owners and use stock in order to change ownership or raise money. Compared to other structures Corporations require more recordkeeping and reporting.
- **Limited Liability Company**: An LLC combines the benefits of a corporation and partnership structure. If your company is sued or declares bankruptcy, you personal assets are secure, unless you've made personal guarantees to your debtors.

When thinking about which entity to select, keep in mind how the ownership, liability and taxes affect you. Also keep in mind that while many startups choose the LLC entity structure, it may be prudent to consult an attorney or accountant for your specific situation.

SBA.gov Business Comparison Chart[5]

Business structure	Ownership	Liability	Taxes
Sole proprietorship	One person	Unlimited personal liability	Personal tax only
Partnerships	Two or more people	Unlimited personal liability unless structured as a limited partnership	Self-employment tax (except for limited partners) Personal tax
Limited liability company (LLC)	One or more people	Owners are not personally liable	Self-employment tax
Corporation - C corp	One or more people	Owners are not personally liable	Corporate tax
Corporation - S corp	One or more people, but no more than 100, and all must be U.S. citizens	Owners are not personally liable	Personal tax
Corporation - B corp	One or more people	Owners are not personally liable	Corporate tax
Corporation - Nonprofit	One or more people	Owners are not personally liable	Tax-exempt, but corporate profits can't be distributed

Brainstorm and Finalize Entity Names

Now that you've selected what legal entity structure best suits your startup, it's time to think about what to call your company. You also want to think about what, if any, trade names you may need. Many startup entrepreneurs get distracted with choosing a name first, then doing everything else. Thinking of names is fun, but be careful not to lose focus.

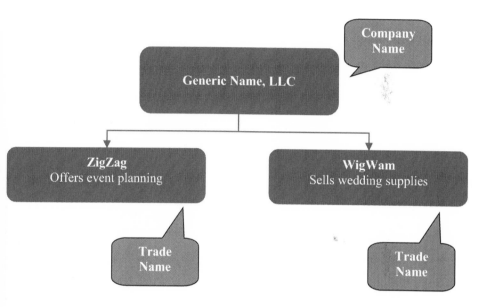

There can be a difference between your company name and your trade name. Let's assume that your company is Generic Name, LLC. You can choose to do business or "trade as" Generic Name, LLC, or you can choose a trade name, such as WigWam. Some companies have multiple trade names, which offer multiple different products or services registered under the same Company Name.

Keep in mind that trade names are not a requirement and often use for marketing or diversification of product purposes.

In order to select your company or trade name you must first check with your state of registration to make sure the names are not being used by another company in your state. Many states offer this service online.

Pick a company name that explains or at least hints at what your startup does. A name like ZigZag or WigWam is actually a terrible company name, because your potential consumers have no idea if your products or services relate to their needs and wants. Keep in mind that you may not have access to capital that can help drive your branding campaign, so keep it simple. Names like ZigZag Marketing or WigWam IT Supply immediately advertise what you're offering.

Drafting the Articles of Organization/Incorporation

The type of entity you've selected will dictate what type of "Articles" you'll have to file with your state government. For example, if you've elected to form a Limited Liability Company (LLC), you'll file an Articles of Organization. Other entity types and article filing types are as follows:

Corporation = Articles of Incorporation
Sole Proprietorship = Application for Sole Proprietorship

There are more breakdowns, however, how the breakdowns occur depend heavily on the state in which you'll be filing.

There are two ways for you to draft your articles or application. First, you can fill out the generic form that the state government provides on their

---

ARTICLES OF ORGANIZATION

The undersigned, with the intention of creating a Maryland Limited Liability Company files the following Articles of Organization:

(1) The name of the Limited Liability Company is: _____

_____

_____

(2) The purpose for which the Limited Liability Company is filed is as follows: _____

_____

_____

(3) The address of the Limited Liability Company in Maryland is _____

_____

(4) The resident agent of the Limited Liability Company in Maryland is _____

_____

whose address is _____

_____

(5) _____   (6) _____
                                          Resident Agent

_____
       Signature(s) of Authorized Person(s)

Filing party's return address:

(7) _____

_____

_____

_____

A generic "Articles of Organization" posted on Maryland's State Department of Assessments and Taxation website.

website or in their office. The below is an example of a state's generic[6] Articles of Organization for a Limited Liability Company. This is a perfectly acceptable method for many startups to quickly and cost effectively draft articles or applications.

The second method is to have an attorney draft your Articles of Organization or Incorporation and file them for you. Consider this method if your entity is more complicated, with stock offerings and multiple partners. Attorneys can also draft your articles in such a way to register multiple trade names, saving you money.

Trade Names can be registered at any time by completing a Trade Name Application with your state of choice. Trade names can be registered to individuals (sole proprietorships) or companies such as LLCs or Corporations.

Remember that every state has regulations stipulating that changes of address, name, ownership or resident agency must be filed with the state. Each state has different methods for submitting changes and different timelines.

Now that your Articles or Applications are drafted, it's time to file them. There are typically four methods to file your paperwork.

- **In-Person**: The quickest option is to go into a state office, file your paperwork in person and have your startup registered immediately.
- **Online**: Many states offer this option and the registration turnaround time is typically about seven business days or less.
- **By Fax**: Another relatively quick option is faxing your articles to the state office. This registration turnaround time is also typically about seven business days or less.
- **By Mail**: The slowest turnaround time comes with mailing in your articles to be filed, which typically takes about six to eight weeks.

After filing, you will wait to receive written confirmation that your entity registration has been accepted and recorded with the state. It's very important to keep any confirmation documents provided to you by the state as you will need them for many of the next steps.

Applying for a FEIN with the IRS

A Federal Employee Identification Number or FEIN (also referred to as EIN) is how the Internal Revenue Service identifies your company. Every FEIN is unique to a singular entity so companies with similar or the same names can be treated separately. The FEIN can be considered somewhat the same as a person's social security number, which identifies them to the IRS.

What you'll need to apply for an FEIN is your state confirmation letters and the personal information of all the members or owners of your startup.

Once you've gather this information there are three ways to file for an EIN.

- **Online**: The IRS website permits you to file an online application and immediately received an EIN confirmation letter.
- **By Phone**: Business owners are able to call the IRS and speak with a customer representative to file for their EIN. The confirmation letter will be mailed to you.
- **By Mail**: You will mail the application to the IRS and the IRS will mail you a confirmation letter.

Regardless of your method of filing, remember to save and have multiple copies of your EIN confirmation letter. Treat this like you do your social security card.

Apply for State Government Account Numbers

Similar to applying for an IRS EIN, different states have different requirements for tax identification numbers. Although these vary state by state, there are some common identification numbers which you'll need.

- **Withholding Tax**: If you're planning on being an employer, then you'll need a tax withholding account. You'll withhold taxes from your employees, and then pay that withholding to the state government. In many case, you'll also match the withholding.

- **Unemployment Tax**: Similarly if you're planning on being an employer, then you'll need an unemployment insurance account. States require you to pay a certain amount of money for each employee, in case they ever file for unemployment.
- **Sales and Use Tax**: If you are involved with selling to consumers directly, then you'll likely need a sales and use tax account number, so you can collect sales tax from consumers and provide it to the government.

Businesses are a major source of tax collection for both state and federal governments. The diagram below should help in understanding this relationship. Your tax accountant can go into further details of your specific situation.

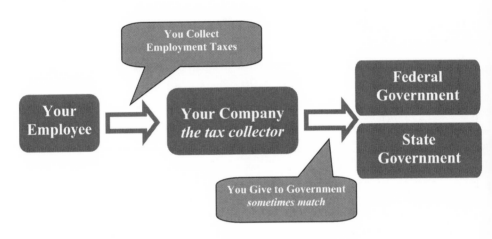

Applying for Local/County Government Account Numbers

Many local jurisdictions require you to obtain additional licenses to conduct business in their city or county. For example, counties may require special business licenses for mechanics, retail shops, construction companies or home businesses. Make sure to check with your city or county, by contacting your town hall or courthouse.

Applying for Special State/Federal Trade License or Permits

Similarly, states and even the federal government may require you to obtain special licenses to conduct specialized trades. While every state is different, there are some general trades that require some level of special licensing.

- Home Improvement License
- Door to Door Salesperson License
- Electrician License
- Gas Fitter License
- HVAC License
- Mechanical License
- Plumber License
- Home Inspector License
- Taxicabs
- Utility Contractor License
- Auctioneer License
- Huckster License
- Pawnbroker License
- Roadside Vendor Permit
- Taxicab Operator License
- Tow Company License
- Second Hand Dealer License

- Daycare Permit
- Consignment Goods Dealer License
- Employment Agency License
- Junk Dealer License
- Ticket Agency License
- Retail Motor Fuel License
- Bowling Alley Permit
- Dance Academy Permit
- Halls or Sport Center Permit
- Motion Picture Theater License
- Liquor License
- Live Entertainment License
- Tattooing License
- Hair Dresser License
- Esthetician License
- Massage Therapist License

If your startup falls within any of these categories, make sure to contact the appropriate state agency to find out about licensing requirements. Typically the state department of labor regulates these types of licenses, however, your state may be different.

Remember that just because your business type is not on this list, does not mean it doesn't require a special license. Contact your state government to find out.

Identifying Eligibility for State or Federal Special Business Certifications

The Federal as well as State governments have special business certification programs which aim to provide assistance or special contracts for certain business whose ownership is considered special. Some of these special certifications include:

- **Woman Owned Businesses**: State and Federal governments set out specific percentages of government contracts for businesses which are certified to be majority woman-owned and operated.

- **Minority Owned Businesses** State and Federal governments set out specific percentages of government contracts for businesses which are certified to be majority minority-person owned and operated.

- **Disabled Owned Businesses:** State and Federal governments set out specific percentages of government contracts for businesses which are certified to be majority disabled-person owned and operated.

- **Veteran Owned Businesses**: State and Federal governments set out specific percentages of government contracts for businesses which are certified to be majority armed forces veteran owned and operated.

- **Locally Owned Businesses:** Local governments set out specific percentages of government contracts for businesses which are certified to be majority owned and operated by residents of a particular county or city.

- **8a Certification:** The Federal government's program for businesses which are majority owned by minority-persons involves several years of mentoring and special contract set-asides.

- **HubZone Certification**: The Federal government designates certain regions of the country and economically disadvantaged. Businesses with physical locations and employees whom reside in these zones are offered special contracts not available to other businesses.

The registration for these types of certifications is very complicated and cannot be covered under one chapter. Look for a special edition of "The Startup King", called **"The Startup King": Special Business Certifications**, which discusses eligibility and advantages of these certifications in depth.

Need for Trademark or Patent Registration

If your company is offering a product or service with a specialized and unique process, then you should consider contacting an intellectual property attorney to review requirements for permits. Similarly, if you are selling a product with a unique name or would like to protect your business or product name against usage by other businesses, contact an attorney to begin a trademark application.

Patents and trademarks are regulated by the US Patent and Trademark Office.

5

Financial Platform

Setting up your business's financial platform will likely come immediately after receiving your IRS EIN confirmation letter. With all confirmation letters and ownership information in-hand, you're ready to open a bank account.

Setting up Financial Platforms Checklist

- ☐ Select Preferred Financial Institution(s)
    - o Bank
    - o Credit Cards
- ☐ Collect Name / Address / Social Security Number / Driver's License Copy of ALL Members of Entity
- ☐ Collect Articles of Organization and FEIN Confirmation Letter
- ☐ Present Collected Information to Preferred Bank
    - o Setup Deposit Account
    - o Setup Payment Account
    - o Setup Payroll Liability Account
- ☐ Order Checks
    - o Select Check Requirements Based on Operations Agreement
        - ▪ i.e. Number of Signature Lines / Limits for 1 vs. 2 Signatures
- ☐ Apply for Credit Cards with Preferred Institution
    - o Confirm Number of Credits, Credit Limits, Credit Cards for Individual Employees
- ☐ Apply for Line of Credit (LOC) with Preferred Institution

Selecting a Bank and Credit Card

There are two way to approach the selection of banks or credit cards. First, you can stay with the banks and credit card companies that conduct your personal financial transactions. This is beneficial if you have established a relationship with your local bank and have a good history with your personal bank and credit card companies. These factors may land you better rates.

The other option and especially if you're not tied to staying with your personal bank, would be to shop around for the best bank and credit cards. As a startup you should look for institutions which offer business checking accounts with no monthly or opening fees. It's also preferable to go with an institution which doesn't required minimum balances.

Many banks which offer free checking accounts do so by limiting the number of transactions you can make in a month. Make sure this limit is acceptable to your business activities.

Once you've selected which bank suits your needs, you'll need the following items to open a bank account:

1. State registrations confirmation letter
2. State trade name confirmation letters
3. IRS EIN confirmation letter
4. Copies of driver's licenses for all owners
5. Social security numbers for all owners

Preparing this information ahead of time for the bank representative will speed up the process.

Many businesses, especially those with multiple employees, decide to setup three accounts at the outset of the company. These three accounts include

1. A deposit account, which will be used to deposit member contributions and revenue from sales
2. A payment account, which will be used to pay bills and debts

3. A payroll liability account, which will be used to pay taxes and contributions owned to the state and federal government

Keep in mind that this is not a requirement and is done so for organization purposes only. All deposits and payments can be made from one bank account.

Ordering Checks

It is always recommended not to order checks, other than a starter set, from your bank. The checks offered at banks come from third parties and are almost always more expensive than going direct to a check printing company.

When ordering your checks make sure to consider how many signature lines are required, based on your operations agreements, and if there are any restrictions on the sum of the check.

Applying for Credit Cards with Preferred Institution

Shopping for the best rate and benefits in a credit card for your business is very important. Use the following factors to make your decision

- o Does the credit limit offered suit your needs?
- o What is the process for future credit limit increases?
- o Are there fees for ordering additional credit cards for employees?
- o Is online banking offered at no charge?
- o What financial software packages sync with the online banking?
- o Does the credit card offer special offers or benefits like cash back?

Remember to take on only the credit limits that you need and do not overextend your business with credit debt.

Apply for Line of Credit (LOC) with Preferred Institution

Your bank may offer the opening of a Line of Credit when you open a bank account. This depends on your assets, type of business, credit history and many other factors. Apply for an LOC only if you need it. Often manufacturing businesses or other production companies apply for LOCs just in case they may need it in times between large payments.

6

Financial Software

With your bank and credit cards selected and checking accounts in hand it's now time to setup your financial software. Although it is possible to maintain small business finances using manual paper and pen methods, it is highly advisable to use some kind of financial software. Benefits of software include the ability to print financial reports with ease, ability to download transactions from banks and credit cards online, efficiency and accuracy.

Setting up Financial Software Checklist

- ☐ Select Accounting/Bookkeeping Software
  - o Does Industry Require Specialized Software?
- ☐ Select Appropriate Software Load (Retail, B2B, Service, Wholesale, etc.)
- ☐ Input Entity Information
  - o Entity Name/Type
  - o Entity Tax Filing Type
  - o Owners/Members
  - o Annual Reporting Dates
  - o FEIN

Selecting Accounting/Bookkeeping Software

There are many accounting software packages out there and you should take the time to research as many as possible. You can also discuss preferences with your tax accountant. Some of these packages include:

- QuickBooks
- Sage
- Fresh Books
- Wave

- Xero
- Microsoft Dynamics
- Bill.com
- Account Edge
- Less Accounting
- Kashoo

Consider these questions when selecting your software:

1. What is the initial cost?
2. Are there update costs?
3. How often does the software get updated?
4. Are there extra costs for processing paychecks and payroll liabilities?
5. Does your tax professional or accountant know how to use the software?
6. What are the software's customer reviews on ease and reliability?

Always consider if the software meets specific industry requirements. For example, will the software tailor its Chart of Accounts to your construction or consulting companies? Will it be able to customize to your retail business?

If you are a specialized government contractor, different agencies such as a Department of Defense may require you to have specialized accounting software packages which meet strict auditing requirements.

Select Load and Input Entity Information

Once in hand and installed on your computer, software packages will direct you in the setup of your business. The process typically begins with selecting what type of business you have. Once this is done make sure to have the following information to complete the setup.

- o Entity Name/Type
- o Entity Tax Filing Type
- o Owners/Members
- o Annual Reporting Dates

- o FEIN Account
- o Withholding Account
- o Unemployment Insurance Account
- o Sales and Use Tax Account

Make sure to either contact a business consultant with experience to help you with financial software, or be sure to put yourself through formalized or informal training. Things will go wrong with the software and entries and you'll need someone to rely on to troubleshoot.

7

Payroll

Related to setting up financial software is the setup of your payroll software or service. Many of the financial software packages noted previously offer add-on payroll services. The question is are you ready and able to do this yourself, or will you outsource payroll to a payroll processing company. To provide you a better understanding of this process, let's assume that you will do this yourself.

Setting up Payroll Service or Software Checklist

- ☐ Input Employer Status Information
    - o FEIN
    - o State Withholding Accounts (May be Multiple States)
    - o State Unemployment Accounts (May be Multiple States)
    - o State Sales/Use Tax Accounts (May be Multiple States)
- ☐ Prepare List of Payroll Liability Reports with Due Dates
- ☐ Prepare List of Payroll Liability Payments with Due Dates
- ☐ Enter Employees into Payroll System (Based on New Employee Forms)

Input Employer Status Information

After selecting the software to use for payroll paycheck and payroll liability payments, you'll input relevant information into the software. If you need a refresher on payroll liability taxes are and the reasons they are collected, look back to the Entity Formation Chapter of this book.

Preparing Payroll Liability Report and Payment List

It is very important for you to understand what payroll liability reports and payments are assigned to your business. Every business can be different depending on the type and location(s) of registration. Some businesses will be responsible to file for multiple states. Some states will not require the filing of some taxes, such as Florida and Withholding tax. Conduct your research and use the table below to help you organize what, when and how you will file and pay.

The first three rows for standard federal taxes have been filled out for you as an example. Even if you choose to have a third party complete your payroll check and payroll liability filings, this information is import for you to know and retain.

Keep in mind that Filing and Payment frequencies will depend on the size of your business, number of employees and other state regulations.

Payroll Liability Filing and Payment Table

Type of Tax	Tax Form and Title	Filing Frequency	Filing Method	Payment Frequency	Payment Method
W2s/W3s	Wage and Tax Statement Transmittal	Annually	eFile	n/a	n/a
Federal Unemployment	940: Employer's Annual Federal Unemployment	Annually	Mail-In	Quarterly	ePay
Federal Withholding	941: Employer's Quarterly Federal Tax Return	Quarterly	Mail-In	Semi-Weekly	ePay
State 1 Unemployment					
State 1 Withholding					
State 1 Sales & Use					

49

Enter Employees into Payroll System

Regardless of whether you'll be conducting payroll yourself or outsourcing it to a third party, you'll need to collect specific information from employees to input into your software or third party software.

The minimum information typically required is the following:

1. Contact Information
2. Tax Information, including social security number
3. Date of Birth
4. Copies of Driver's License or Identification
5. Copies of proof of citizenship or permanent residency ("green card")
6. An employee completed IRS Form W-4
7. An employee completed ICE Form I-9
8. An employee completed state form for withholding tax

To download a New Hire Form template, W-4s, I-9s, state withholding tax forms and many other helpful templates, visit to ww.sonofmedia.com and look under "The Startup King."

Third Party Payroll Services

If you're interested in third party payroll services, research ADP, PayChex, Zenefits, Custo, Patriot Payroll or APS Payroll, to mention a few.

8

Insurance

To protect your business assets as well as your personal assets, it is highly recommend that a business invest in insurance. Small side hustles will typically not require insurance depending on the level and type of activity; however, it is still recommended that you obtain quotes.

Of course, keep in mind that you may not have a choice depending on the type of business you plan to operate. In many cases, you are required by law to maintain a certain level of insurance.

Setting up Insurance Checklist

- ☐ Identify Insurance Required
- ☐ Request Quotes and Finalize Insurance Purchase
  - o Business Liability Insurance
  - o Business Property Insurance
  - o Business Vehicle Insurance
  - o Worker's Compensation
  - o Specialized Industry Insurance?
  - o Employee Health Insurance
  - o Temporary Disability Insurance (CA)

Identify Insurance Required

There are many types of insurance that can be purchase or required by law depending on where you operate. These are some common insurance types across industries and borders:

1. Business Liability Insurance
2. Business Property Insurance
3. Business Vehicle Insurance
4. Worker's Compensation
5. Employee Health Insurance

Does your State require you to have a special insurance? For example, California requires that businesses have Temporary Disability Insurance. Also consider if your specialized industry requires a certain type of insurance or insurance limit.

Requesting Insurance Quotes

It is a great idea to receive at least three quotes for every type of insurance. Be sure to meet with an insurance agent in person and ask as many questions as possible. These are the experts that know insurance, insurance regulation and insurance requirements. Of course, they will try to sell you, but it will be up to you to double check their statements against your research.

When purchasing insurance, consider asking these questions :

1. What are industry minimum requirements for insurance?
2. What limits do you recommend?
3. If I choose your company, who do I contact with questions?
4. How well is your insurance company rated?
5. How quickly will you provide me with a Certificate of Insurance after a request has been issued?

9

Administrative Procedures

It is very important for startup entrepreneurs to understand the administrative flow of their business. This function of small business can typically be divided into three categories: accounts payable for vendors, accounts receivable for customers and finally, employees.

Setting up Administrative Procedures Checklist

- ☐ Accounts Payable
    - ○ Purchase Orders
    - ○ Receiving Inventory/Merchandise
    - ○ Entering Bills
    - ○ Paying Bills
- ☐ Accounts Receivable
    - ○ Estimating
    - ○ Invoices / Account Statements
    - ○ Contracts? Service Agreements?
    - ○ Payments
        - ▪ Checks/Credit Cards/Credit Terms
    - ○ Receiving Payments and Collections
    - ○ Recording Deposits

Here is a diagram of a typical administrative structure of a small business. The top boxes concern vendors and the bottom boxes concern customers.

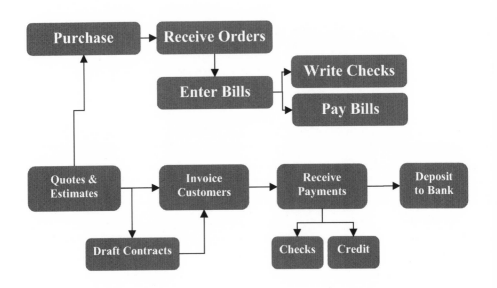

Setting Up Accounts Payable

The accounts payable function involves your businesses' relationship with vendors. Accounts payables typically include these four areas:

1. **Purchase Orders**: A document informing a vendor of your desire to place and order, specifying the date of order, items to be ordered, prices agreed upon, payment terms, lead times quoted and other details.

2. **Receiving Inventory/Merchandise**: After your purchase order has been received and processed by your vendor, your will received the items ordered. You must enter receipt of these against your purchase order.

3. **Entering Bills**: Your vendors will also send you a bill once items ship to your location. Other vendors such as landlords, phone

companies, gas, companies, etc. will also send you bills. You should enter these bills into your account software to sort by due date. You can also write checks without bills, although it is not standard practice.

4. **Paying Bills**: When it's time to pay the bills you can do so in your accounting software and a check will be generated for you to print. You can also manually write these checks.

Setting Up Accounts Receivable

This is why most people start businesses, to make money! The accounts receivable function involves your business's relationship with customers. Accounts receivable typically includes these six areas:

1. **Estimating**: You will provide quotes and estimates to your customers based on services or products they need. Some businesses, such as retail, will provide this area in the form of price tags.

2. **Invoices**: If an estimate or quote is accepted, typically an invoice is generated. Invoices generated before a product or project is completed are used to receive deposits.

3. **Contracts or Service Agreements**: Your business may require additional paperwork before an invoice is created if the type of work you do is more complicated and requires terms of agreement for completing work. Construction companies, manufacturing, consulting are some industries where this applies.

4. **Payments**: You will receive partial or full payments via check, credit card or cash (not recommended). Remember to consider providing customers payment terms to encourage them to pay more quickly and to make your business more competitive.

5. **Receiving Payments and Collections**: In unfortunate circumstances, there are times when a customer will not pay and must be motivated to meet their obligations. Make sure you

understand collections laws in your state and have a collections process, with standardized letters to start this process.

6. **Recording Deposits**: After you take your payments to the bank to be deposited, make sure those deposits are recorded in your financial software.

10

Marketing

The marketing of your business or services is more than just coming up with ideas or creating eye-catching logos. This is a complicated subject and requires an entire book to cover this subject in detail. In fact, be on the lookout for **"The Startup King": Real Marketing.**

Setting up Marketing Checklist

- ☐ Finalize Marketing Strategy
- ☐ Create Logo
- ☐ Business Cards
- ☐ Letterhead
- ☐ Envelopes
- ☐ Register Domain/URL
- ☐ Create Website
- ☐ Create Email Accounts
- ☐ Create Social Media Accounts

Finalize Marketing Strategy

Using the information you developed during writing your business plan, including identifying trends and patterns with your target market, as well as the methods of channels that would be most effectively used to reach your target market, you can now finalize a marketing strategy.

Your marketing strategy will reiterate who your target market is and how you will reach them. You may divide your target market based on different products or based on different marketing mediums and vehicles to reach them. It's also important to finish your marketing strategy before creating marketing media or advertising, because you need to have a clear understand of what exactly you want to advertise.

The same rule applies as writing a business plan, DO NOT write a lengthy document that takes up all of your time. Stay concise and outline.

Creating a Logo

Your logo doesn't have to be something fancy. Use colors and symmetry to create something eye catching. It's nice to be able to incorporate your logo into the name of your company, especially a name that tells consumers what you do. Don't spend countless hours on a logo as a startup. There are more important things to which you can dedicate your time.

Registering your Domain Name

In today's climate there are many companies from Google to GoDaddy that register domain names. It's cheap and easy to register and a necessity in order to be competitive. Keep it as simple as possible and consider that it must be printable and advertising ready.

Creating Email Accounts

If you have the means it is highly desirable to have email accounts created in the name of your business, rather than using a generic @gmail or @yahoo email account. This adds professionalism to your startup and may set it apart from competition. You can also pay for Gmail or Outlook web-based platforms to not have to deal with bland, generic email platforms.

Printing Business Cards

With your logo, domain and email in hand, you're ready to print business cards. Make sure to shop around online and find the best deal. Full color business cards are highly attractive, but generic cards are often less costly. Pick what suits your needs and resources.

Printing Stationary: Letterheads, Envelopes, etc.

Unless you're a larger startup, the need for letterheads and customizable stationary is non-existent. If you are a larger startup, do some online shopping to find the best quality and pricing.

Creating a Website

There are many do-it-yourself services for website building. If you require a website for informational purposes only, these sources are fine and inexpensive. If you require a catchy website which needs to updated routinely, requires customizable graphics, then research web developers to create a website for you. Often, you can find younger companies or individuals who create phenomenal websites for cheaper than established companies. Why not support other side hustlers?

Creating Social Media Accounts

Before creating your *Facebook, Twitter or Instagram* accounts, ask yourself two questions. First, do I really need this account? Consider if having a social media account really adds value to your business. Second, ask yourself if you will have the time to routinely update your social media. Social media feeds that have not been updated in a while present a very poor image of a successful business.

11

Facilities

When you're not running a side hustle and not using your home office as your physical work location, you'll need to locate and finalize a physical location for your business. This can be a retail, warehouse and office or combination space.

Setting up Facilities Checklist

- Determine Initial Business/Office Location Needs
  - o Determine Minimum Requirements of Space
- Contact Commercial Real Estate Agents with Requirements
  - o Select Space(s)
  - o Check Zoning Compliance
  - o Check Local/County Standards Compliance
  - o Review Lease Terms and Price
  - o Review and Finalize Lease
  - o Receive Certificate of Occupancy
- Fixtures
  - o Identify Necessary Furniture
  - o Signage
  - o Equipment?
  - o Office Supplies
  - o IT / Computers
  - o Phones

Determining Initial Business/Office Location Needs

At this point you should be very familiar with the requirements of your business, having done an extensive level of planning. When considering locations, you must consider several factors:

1. Do you need to be in a certain neighborhood? Close to clients or target market?
2. Do you need retail, office, warehouse or a combination?
3. What is the minimum amount of space you can use to conduct your business?

Contact Commercial Real Estate Agents with Requirements

Commercial agents act as intermediaries between property owners and lessees. Just as it is important for you to have an agent when purchasing a home, it is important for you to have a commercial agent when leasing a commercial space. Your interests must be protected by people who do this on a daily basis.

Be prepared to discuss all of the following requirements with your commercial agent, so that they may find the desire space as quickly as possible.

1. **Zoning Compliance**: If you are leasing space to conduct retail activities, make sure your space is zoned by the local government as retail space. If not, you will waste a lot of time and money.
2. **Lease Terms and Price**: What can you afford? Also consider the future of the business and be sure to request advantageous "Options to Renew" in the initial lease terms. You can also request that the landlord provide you with a sum to make improvements or defer several months rent so you can make the improvements yourself.

Once you have secured your lease, made any renovations, you will be ready to apply for a certificate of occupancy from your local government.

Be sure to research the requirements for an occupancy permit prior to signing the lease.

Fixtures

Make sure you consider the fixtures you'll need when signing the lease. This also should also be in your business plan under the budget. The list of fixtures below are common items that are common in every business.

1. **Furniture**: Desks, chairs, lighting, etc.
2. **Signage**: Do you need custom signage and does zoning permit for it?
3. **Equipment**: Do you require specialized equipment?
4. **Office Supplies**
5. **IT / Computers:** Consider your needs and start with the minimum that you need. Perhaps outsource server storage until you have enough money.
6. **Internet/Phones**: Try to save on phone by using cell phones or VOIP.

Undoubtedly there are more items that you will need. Remember, as has been said before, every business has unique features. Do your research, know your business.

The Startup Dream Begins

Starting a business involves a lot of technical elements. You may need to review the contents of this book several times, and consult other sources. Don't get discouraged by the amount of paperwork required.

If you pick the best type of business that suits you, your interests and passions, the resources available to you, and if you do things correctly from the beginning, it will be a much more enjoyable process.

So whether you decide to go with a Side Hustle, be a Big Spender or form your startup from the Group Up, please do not hesitate to contact me if you have any questions or need clarification on anything discussed, or not, in this book.

Also be sure to stay tuned for these future guides, with more practice help and advice:

☐ **The Startup King: Special Business Certifications**
☐ **The Startup King: Human Resources for Small Business**
☐ **The Startup King: Real Marketing**

I wish you the best of luck in pursuing your piece of the American Dream.

"The Startup King's" Checklist

Pre-Planning

- ☐ Write Business Plan
  - o Write Marketing Strategy (Part of Business Plan)
- ☐ Draft Operations Agreement (if partnership)

Formation of Entity

- ☐ Select Entity Registration State
  - o Identify Resident Agent(s)
- ☐ Select Entity Type
  - o Sole Proprietorship
  - o Partnership
  - o Corporation
  - o C Corporation / S Corporation / B Corporation
  - o Limited Liability Company
- ☐ Select Post LLC Formation Filing Status
  - ▪ C-Corp OR S-Corp
- ☐ Brainstorm Entity Names
  - o Also Brainstorm "Trade" Names (if applicable)
  - o Check Entity Name Availability with State
  - o Check Entity Trade Name Availability with State
  - o Finalize Names
- ☐ Draft Articles of Organization
  - o File Articles of Organization (In Person, Online, Fax)
  - o Wait for Confirmation of Acceptance
- ☐ Apply for FEIN with IRS
- ☐ Apply for State Government Account Numbers
  - o State Withholding Tax Number
  - o State Unemployment Tax Number
  - o State Sales/Use Tax Number (if/when applicable)
- ☐ Apply for Local/County Government Account Numbers
  - o Business License Permit
- ☐ Identify Need for Special State/Federal Trade License or Permit
  - o Begin Process if Applicable (May Require Attorney)

- ☐ Identify Eligibility for State/Federal Special Business Certifications to Qualify for Special Access
- ☐ Identify Need for Trademark or Patent Registration (Requires Attorney)
- ☐ Foreign Corporation Registrations in Other States

Setting up Financial Platforms

- ☐ Select Preferred Financial Institution(s)
  - o Bank
  - o Credit Cards
- ☐ Collect Name / Address / Social Security Number / Driver's License Copy of ALL Members of Entity
- ☐ Collect Articles of Organization and FEIN Confirmation Letter
- ☐ Present Collected Information to Preferred Bank
  - o Setup Deposit Account
  - o Setup Payment Account
  - o Setup Payroll Liability Account
- ☐ Order Checks
  - o Select Check Requirements Based on Operations Agreement
    - ▪ i.e. Number of Signature Lines / Limits for 1 vs. 2 Signatures
- ☐ Apply for Credit Cards with Preferred Institution
  - o Confirm Number of Credits, Credit Limits, Credit Cards for Individual Employees
- ☐ Apply for Line of Credit (LOC) with Preferred Institution

Setting up Financial Software

- ☐ Select Accounting/Bookkeeping Software
  - o Does Industry Require Specialized Software?
- ☐ Select Appropriate Software Load (Retail, B2B, Service, Wholesale, etc.)
- ☐ Input Entity Information
  - o Entity Name/Type
  - o Entity Tax Filing Type
  - o Owners/Members
  - o Annual Reporting Dates
  - o FEIN

Setting up Payroll Service or Software

- ☐ Input Employer Status Information
  - ○ FEIN
  - ○ State Withholding Accounts (May be Multiple States)
  - ○ State Unemployment Accounts (May be Multiple States)
  - ○ State Sales/Use Tax Accounts (May be Multiple States)
- ☐ Prepare List of Payroll Liability Reports with Due Dates
- ☐ Prepare List of Payroll Liability Payments with Due Dates
- ☐ Enter Employees into Payroll System (Based on New Employee Forms)

Setting up Insurance

- ☐ Identify Insurance Required
- ☐ Request Quotes and Finalize Insurance Purchase
  - ○ Business Liability Insurance
  - ○ Business Property Insurance
  - ○ Business Vehicle Insurance
  - ○ Worker's Compensation
  - ○ Specialized Industry Insurance?
  - ○ Employee Health Insurance
  - ○ Temporary Disability Insurance (CA)

Setting up Administrative Procedures

- ☐ Accounts Payable
  - ○ Purchase Orders
  - ○ Receiving Inventory/Merchandise
  - ○ Entering Bills
  - ○ Paying Bills
- ☐ Accounts Receivable
  - ○ Estimating
  - ○ Invoices / Account Statements
  - ○ Contracts? Service Agreements?
  - ○ Payments
    - ▪ Checks/Credit Cards/Credit Terms
  - ○ Receiving Payments and Collections
  - ○ Recording Deposits

Setting up Marketing

- ☐ Finalize Marketing Strategy
- ☐ Create Logo
- ☐ Business Cards
- ☐ Stationary, Letterhead, Envelopes
- ☐ Register Domain/URL
- ☐ Create Website
- ☐ Create Email Accounts
- ☐ Create Social Media Accounts

Setting up Facilities

- ☐ Determine Initial Business/Office Location Needs
  - o Determine Minimum Requirements of Space
- ☐ Contact Commercial Real Estate Agents with Requirements
  - o Select Space(s)
  - o Check Zoning Compliance
  - o Check Local/County Standards Compliance
  - o Review Lease Terms and Price
  - o Review and Finalize Lease
  - o Receive Certificate of Occupancy
- ☐ Fixtures
  - o Identify Necessary Furniture
  - o Signage
  - o Equipment
  - o Office Supplies
  - o IT / Computers
  - o Phones

STARTUP NOTES

STARTUP NOTES

STARTUP NOTES

STARTUP NOTES

STARTUP NOTES

End Notes

[1] World Bank. Doing Business 2017: Measuring Business Regulations, Economy Rankings. Rease of Doing Business Rank. Found at: http://www.doingbusiness.org/rankings

[2] Entrepreneur.com. "Jeff Bezos The King of E-Commerce." October 10, 2008. Found at: https://www.entrepreneur.com/article/197608

[3] The Small Business Administration (SBA). "Write Your Business Plan." Found at: https://www.sba.gov/business-guide/plan/write-your-business-plan-template

[4] Michelle Fabio. *legalzoom*. "Starting Up? Which State to File Your LLC In." Found at: https://www.legalzoom.com/articles/starting-up-which-state-to-file-your-llc-in

[5] The Small Business Adminstration (SBA). "Choose a business structure." Found at: https://www.sba.gov/business-guide/launch/choose-business-structure-types-chart

[6] Maryland State Department of Assessments and Taxation (MDSDAT). Taxpayer Services Forms For Businesses. Found at: http://dat.maryland.gov/SDAT%20Forms/artorgan.pdf

34929395R00045

Made in the USA
Middletown, DE
30 January 2019